CRUSTY

And His Red Sweater

Written by Tracy Voss

Illustrated by Marcy Tippmann

Dedicated to my childhood best friend, Bear.

You were always by my side no matter what I was doing, my big black Bear. I was never alone because of you, and you dried many of my tears on your fur. I look for you every time I go to the shelters in search of another black dog that needs a second chance. Without you, I would have been lost and lonely. I won't ever forget you and your unconditional love.

Acknowledgments:

I would like to thank Mary Wright, Cyra Dumitru, and Andrea Ptak— all dog lovers—who helped connect all the pieces together to make this book possible.

Crusty and His Red Sweater—The Amazing Story of a Real-Life Rescue Dog
©2021 Tracy Voss
All rights reserved.
Except for brief excerpts for review purposes, no part of this book may be reproduced or used in any form without written permission from the publisher. For more information about this book or the author, visit LiveLikeaDog.press.

Hardback ISBN 978-1-7377470-0-0
Paperback ISBN 979-8-9864244-0-8
eISBN 978-1-7377470-2-4

First edition 2021
Printed in the United States of America
Live Like a Dog, LLC
PO Box 849
Hondo, TX 78861
LiveLikeaDog.press

Book Designer: Marcy Tippmann
Project Manager: Andrea Leigh Ptak

I know I don't look so great right now but I have to find someone to help me. Someone who loves dogs.

Do you love dogs?

To tell you the truth, I don't feel so great and I am really hungry.

I used to have a family but when they moved away they left me behind in my red sweater. It helps keep me warm because I don't have a lot of fur.

I don't know why they left me behind. I think I am a good dog.

Would you take care of me if I was your dog?

Would you take me with you if you had to move?

Lots of people walk by me but no one stops to help. I think it's because I don't look cute, like other dogs. I am all crusty. But I am a good dog with lots of love to give. I just need some help.

Would you help me if you were here?

I don't have a lot of fur because I have something called mange. Mange is caused by tiny bugs that make your fur fall out. It is very itchy and it makes me scratch, scratch, scratch! I am crusty everywhere from all the scratching and it hurts.

Would you like to see what one of these bugs looks like through a microscope? Ewwwww!

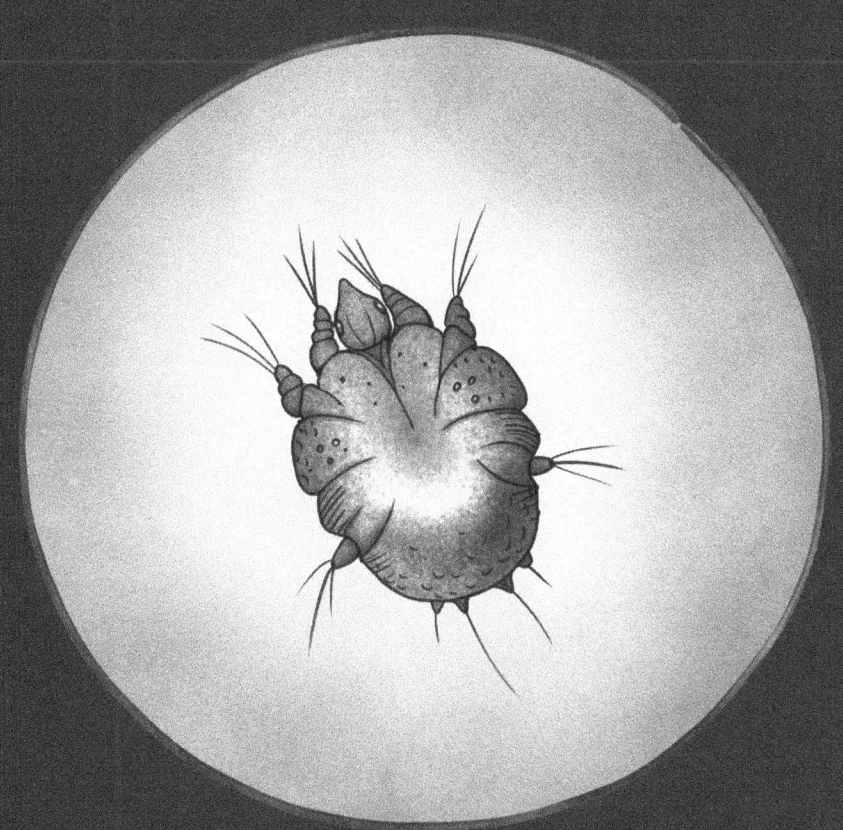

When nighttime comes, I always find a tree to sleep under in case it rains. The dark is scary and I don't like being alone.

Are you afraid of the dark?

Last night I had a dream that someone stopped to help me and she was really nice. When I woke up this morning, guess what?

Rather than walking past me like everyone else, a nice lady stops to say hello. Her name is Tracy and she has lots of dog treats for me. How did she know I was here? How did she know I was hungry? Maybe she has special magical powers?!

Tracy gently picks me up and whispers in my ear, "Everything is going to be OK. You are safe now. I am rescuing you and you're coming with me in my Magic Bus."

Tracy says the first thing we have to do is get all of these yucky bugs off of me. I can't wait!

Can you imagine having bugs crawling all over you? I don't like it at all.

When we arrive at Dr. Bowman's office, they ask Tracy what my name is. She looks at me and says, "Crusty." It is the first name she thinks of because I am crusty all over. I think Crusty is a beautiful name because Tracy picked it.

Dr. Bowman gives me some medicine and tells Tracy to give me baths every day to help my skin get better so that my fur can grow back.

I have never been to a veterinarian before. Tracy says dogs are supposed to visit them once or twice a year for a checkup, just like kids go to the doctor for checkups.

After driving a little further, the Magic Bus stops in front of a rock building with a metal roof. Tracy carries me inside. A sign on the front door says, "Oliver's House."

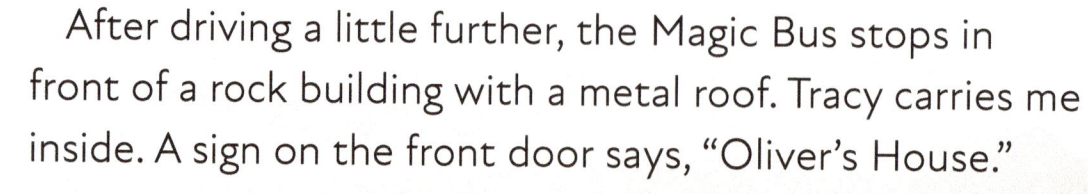

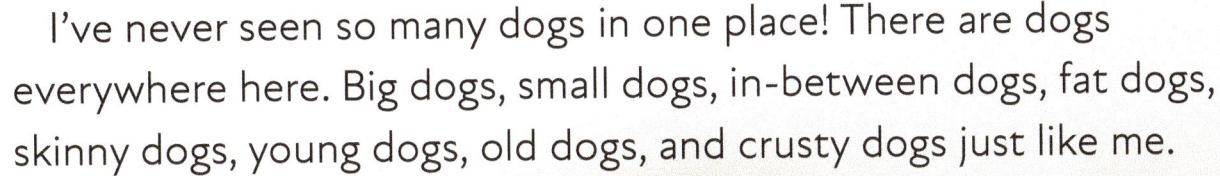

I've never seen so many dogs in one place! There are dogs everywhere here. Big dogs, small dogs, in-between dogs, fat dogs, skinny dogs, young dogs, old dogs, and crusty dogs just like me.

Then, Tracy gives me a wonderful, warm bath. She says I smell bad and so does my red sweater, so we both need to be washed. I've never had a bath before but I really like it.

Do you like to take baths?

After my bath, she puts my red sweater back on because I get cold without it.

I start feeling better right away. Tracy gives me more food to eat and my belly is full for the first time in a very long time. I love it here and I love Tracy!

Before I go to bed at night, Tracy wraps me in a blanket and rocks me in her big rocking chair. She tells me she loves me and gently pets my head. I tell her I love her too and say thank you for helping me.

The only thing I don't like about it here is that I have to share Tracy with so many other dogs. We all want to be rocked in her big rocking chair, but she doesn't have time to rock each of us every day. She is so busy taking care of sick dogs and cleaning up dog poop.

Would you help her pick up the dog poop so she has more time to rock me in her big rocking chair?

Lots of dogs are coming to Oliver's House every day and lots of dogs are leaving every day. Tracy says they are leaving to go to their new homes.

Dogs aren't supposed to live at Oliver's House forever. One day it will be my turn to leave too.

This morning I see myself in the mirror and I can't believe my eyes! All my fur has grown back. I don't look crusty or sick anymore. I think I am quite cute. It's magic here!

Tracy says I don't need my red sweater anymore, either. She takes it off and scratches me all over my back and ears.

Then she tells me I am ready to get adopted.

What? Adopted? I don't want to get adopted.
I want to stay here with Tracy.

Tracy loads me into the Magic Bus with a lot of other dogs, then she starts driving. We drive and drive all night long. She tells us not to be scared. She says that her helpers have picked new families for us who will love us as much as she does.

When the Magic Bus stops, I can hear people outside.
They are waiting for us. Tracy has tears in her eyes—
not because she is sad but because she is happy.

When Tracy hands me to my new mom, Courtney, I know
she is right. When we look at each other, it is love at first sight!
Courtney says she is going to take care of me forever. She
needs me as much as I need her. We rescued each other!

Over the years, I have often thought about Tracy and I will never forget how she helped me when no one else would.

She even came to visit me a few years after I was adopted. She picked me up and whispered in my ear, "I knew you would love Courtney. She loves you as much as I love you. I am so happy you have a home and the best mom in the world to take care of you."

She's right. I am loved, happy, healthy, safe, and I have the best mom in the world!

Crusty was found wandering the streets of Brownsville, Texas wearing his red sweater. He was picked up by Animal Control and taken to the Brownsville shelter where Tracy rescued him.

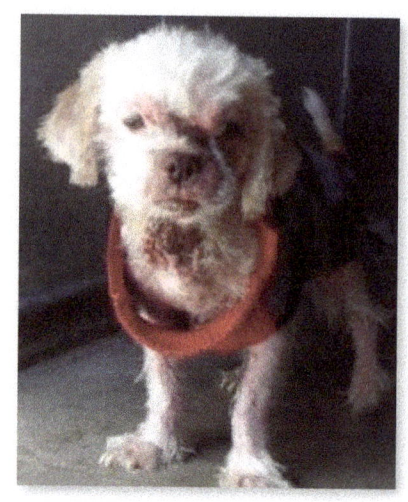

She took him home to her house as her personal foster dog. She took him everywhere with her. He was very sick and his rehabilitation took months of care. After recovering from a severe case of mange and an upper respiratory infection, he was adopted by Courtney in Denver, Colorado on March 15th, 2013.

He was the hardest dog Tracy ever had to adopt out. She became attached to him and didn't want to let him go. Due to the overpopulation problem of stray dogs in South Texas, she knew if she kept him, it would take the spot of another dog that needed her help.

Now, Crusty is a very happy, well taken care of little dog. He was in Courtney's wedding when she got married and is a part of a growing family. He is loved by Courtney, her

mother Nancy, her husband Craig, and their little boy Joshua.

He goes for walks with them and even gets pushed in a dog stroller when he gets tired! He is a loved member of the family and he will never be left behind ever again.

If you see a dog that is wandering around without a home, please tell an adult. All dogs deserve a home where they are taken care of, loved, and have full bellies.

To learn more about Oliver's House, visit us at www.TracysPawsRescue.org

TracysPawsRescue
tracyspawsrescue.org

www.ingramcontent.com/pod-product-compliance
Lightning Source LLC
Chambersburg PA
CBHW041528120626
46551CB00018B/2615